The Burning Heart of a Difference Maker

Simple ways to make a difference in life, relationships, and serving others

Published by
Sam Glenn
Motivational Presentations
608 S Washington Ste 101
Naperville, IL 60540
800-818-6378

Additional copies of this book can be obtained
from any of the authors. Also available at:

www.SamSpeaks.com

Printed in the United States of America

Print and Bind Direct!
Books@PrintAndBind.com

ISBN # 1-881825-34-5

Contents

The Burning Heart of a Difference Maker

Simple ways to make a difference in life, relationships, and serving others.

The purpose of the book is to share the qualities of a difference maker, and share ideas that will make a difference for you. While there are many elements of a difference maker or world changer, my mission is to be simple and get the ball rolling for you. I wish to inspire ideas and thoughts that will get you not just to think about what a difference maker is, but what you can do to make a difference. It is not enough to know what to do; we have to do what we know. All of us count to make a difference! Who you are makes a difference!

This book is a compilation of ideas and thoughts that will inspire you. MY hope is that in the next few pages, you will find the words that inspire to action. A burning heart steps forth into action to impact our world.

Sam Glenn

What is The "Burning Heart" of a Difference Maker?

The "Burning Heart" is in a person who doesn't just sit around and wait for life to happen. They make life happen. They contribute, share, care, give, go, do, and become the core and heart of our world changers.

The "Burning Heart" is a desire, a deep calling to a strong sense of purpose. The heart beats with a mission. Thump! Thump! Thump! Thump! The beating of the heart grows more intense with each passing moment. The blood that passes through the heart is enriched with the thickness of purpose and mission. Thump! Thump! A storehouse of potential, gifts, and talents is just waiting to be used to impact a life, a relationship, a business, and a ministry. The heart beats faster and faster, the temperature gets hotter and hotter, until the difference maker can no longer stand still or remain silent. A person with a burning heart has to do something!

The BIG question:
what is burning in your heart?

There is something within us all that can make a difference in our world. We all have a mark to leave in the world. We all have music within – talents and gifts. Perhaps yours has not been discovered. Perhaps you are afraid to let it out. That is understandable, but you do not have to let your fears get the best of you, or rob the world of your greatness. So what is burning in your heart? What moves you? What inspires you? What is your passion? What do you care enough about to do something about? What is your "Burning Heart"?

The Old Man and the Lady at Wal-Mart

Sam Glenn

"Our People Make the Difference."
–Wal-Mart slogan

A short time ago while shopping in Wal-Mart, I experienced the power of love and the difference it makes. I was standing in the express line with the expectation that it would move quickly. I was wrong. It was taking forever and the line was beginning to build. I looked up at the check-out to see if I could catch a glimpse of what was taking so long. There was an elderly man who was ever so slowly taking his merchandise out of his basket and placing it on the counter. He appeared to be sad by the expression he had on his face and the way he moved his body. He really didn't care that he was holding up the express

1

line. He just went about his business in a sad and slow kind of way.

The other people in line seemed to be getting aggravated, but that still didn't get this man to move any faster. The woman at the check-out counter tried to spark a conversation with him, "Having a good day, sir?"

He didn't even look at her; he kind of just mumbled and continued by paying the woman. As the old man began to walk away, he was hunched over, and dragging his feet. It was not a pretty site, but the woman at the cash register did not let it end there.

She called out to the old man as he was shuffling away, 'Excuse me, sir!"

The old man turned, "Yes?"

"I was wondering, have you had a hug today?"

The old man responded, "No, I have not."

Without hesitation or worrying about all the people waiting for service, the lady walked from behind the counter and embraced the old man in a hug. Not just a hug that says, "Have a good day," but it was an embrace of

2

genuine care and love. It was neat to witness this. The power of genuine care and love began to take its effect. A smile began to appear upon the wrinkled face of the old man. When he turned to walk out, he no longer dragged his feet. His shoulders straightened up and he walked out of there feeling good!!!

The woman walked back behind the counter and served the next customer with a smile, which in turn brought a smile to their face. Everybody in the express line had witnessed something awesome – the power of giving love. The woman behind the counter perhaps earned $7.00 an hour. It was not in her job description to give out hugs to sad people. She didn't get bonuses for each hug given. There was no supervisor around to watch and say, "Good job." There was no expectation on this woman to do anything of such a nature, but she gave what was in her heart. The cost for her to give that hug – nothing; the difference she made – priceless.

"Unless life is lived for others, it is not worthwhile."
    - Mother Teresa

"Your rewards in life are in direct proportion to your service."
    - Earl Nightingale

The Power of One...YOU!

Can one person really make a difference or an impact? Have you ever gone to a major sporting event where over 50,000 people were on hand? It all starts with one crazy nut that does not care about the critics or how weird he or she may seem at first, but the burning fire that rests in their heart can no longer sit still. It burns and burns to the point they just have to do something! They stand to their feet and explode into an enthusiastic cry that sounds like this - "ONE, TWO, THREE! WEEEEE!" Their vision and burning desire is to start the wave. Only a few may join in at first, but that is what leadership is all about. You are going to bring the vision to reality through the help and contribution of others. Again, "ONE, TWO, THREE! WEE!" More join in! Your persistence and belief in the vision finally reaps the reward of the entire stadium doing the wave. And it all started with one simple person who acted on an extraordinary vision.

Making a difference is about joining others in a cause that helps others. They say if you desire to find your real calling and purpose in life, just find something to care about and you will discover your life's great purpose.

Making a difference perhaps is donating your time to make someone else feel better, offering encouragement, love, and hope. Making a difference is giving of yourself to something that will have a real and lasting effect. Making a difference, helping others, and giving of ourselves sows a reward into our inner spirit. You cannot bring light to someone else, without bringing a little to yourself. Les Brown says, "The things you do for yourself will be gone when you are gone, but that which you do for others will remain as your legacy."

What will people remember of you? What is your passion to make a difference? What could you do today that could touch a life? Simply put, leaders have a passion to make a difference. They are the wave makers in the game of life!

"When you speak to others, speak words of life!"

"There are two types of people in this world, the encouragers and the discouragers...one is resented while the other is fondly remembered."

7

The Magic of Kyle

Kathleen Hassan

I have a neighbor named Kyle. He is twelve years old. Born with a reversed chromosome, emotionally, Kyle is about age 6 or 7. When he was very young he would get so frustrated because he couldn't communicate what he wanted. Living right next door, I would hear him scream non-stop for hours on end.

One day, I just couldn't stand it any longer. He'd been crying for almost two hours straight. I finally went over, knocked on the door, told his mother to take a break and asked Kyle if he wanted to go for a walk down to the park. Suddenly and almost miraculously he stopped crying, took my hand and off we went. From that moment on, Kyle and I became best friends.

Little by little, Kyle made progress in school but it was still very difficult for him to communicate. He even learned sign language but no one else in the neighborhood knew it so that really didn't help his situation much. I learned a couple of signs like please and thank you and the most important of all – I love you.

Every time I saw Kyle I would sign I love you and he would give me a giant smile and sign it back.

Then one summer when Kyle was seven, the whole neighborhood came to a screeching halt and a blanket of sadness descended upon us all. Kyle was diagnosed with leukemia. Our annual summer block party was cancelled because no one felt like celebrating without our mascot, Kyle.

He battled for two whole years. He lost his hair, which was almost a blessing because it had always been such a struggle to get his hair cut. He looked adorable with that big, bald, head, those thick glasses and that goofy smile. Ironically, it was during those grueling two years that Kyle's language went through the roof. At the end of those two years Kyle's cancer was in remission.

Just about every day Kyle comes over for a hug. His mother says he needs tactile and sensory stimulation to get centered. Basically he just needs what we all need – love and affection.

One day, I was on a business call with a prospective client. Suddenly, I heard a little knock on the door. "Oh my God," I thought "Not Kyle... Not NOW!"

I held my hand over the receiver and whispered to Kyle that I was on a business call and he'd have to come back later. His little goofy grin turned into the saddest little face I've ever seen. I decided I'd rather lose a client than lose a friend.

I asked the woman if she could please hold for a moment and explained that my friend Kyle had stopped by for his daily hug. I put the phone down, went to the door and gave him the biggest hug in the world. When I got back on the phone, she was so moved that she booked me for the speaking engagement right then and there!

Kyle came over just the other day and gave me a giant hug and said, "I wuv you Ka E" (that's Kyle's version of Kathy - Kathleen would be totally out of the question!)

I said, "Why do you love me so much Kyle?"

He replied, "Because you love me silly."

Difference makers come in all shapes, sizes, ages and abilities. Don't ever be too busy to stop and notice them. They are God's messengers and are sent to remind us that we are indeed loved, silly!

Perseverance Makes a Difference

Gina Waegele

*Perseverance: "To move onward,
no matter what gets in the way."*
- Gina Waegele

Think about the most tragic circumstance in your life. Think about your biggest obstacle. Were you able to overcome the tragedy or the obstacle? Are you currently trying to overcome a particular situation? Think about challenges that may come your way. How will you face them? How will you overcome them?

Life has thrown me some ups and downs. I grew up in a wonderful family, but when I turned 13, tragedy struck. My dad suddenly passed away of a brain aneurysm. Five years later, my freshman year in college, I was in an abusive relationship that left me in the hospital. That same year, my sister Christine was murdered by her own husband. These events plus others, lead me to a deep depression. I got to a point where I had to make a choice on my life. I needed to live or die. I chose to live, but living meant that the only way I was going to make it through the pain and live, was to persevere.

My definition of perseverance is "to move onward no matter what gets in the way." No matter how low I feel, no matter what obstacles are in my way, I choose to move forward and not let the obstacles I face defeat me.

Perseverance makes a difference for you and for others. Because I chose to persevere and make it through the hard times, I have found hope in my life. Every day that I wake up and make the choice to live life to the fullest, I find hope. From the day I chose to persevere and live, each day got easier. Each day I made it through and each day I continue to make it through, I have more hope and more joy.

Choose to live. Choose to persevere through your trials. Only you can make that choice. By persevering, you will find hope and you will give hope to others. When people begin to see your life circumstances and that you have made it through, they will have hope that they can make it through the hard times in their lives. Perseverance makes you stronger and builds your character. Ultimately, it makes a difference in your life and in the lives of others by giving them hope.

"We cannot become what we need to be by remaining what we are."
– Oprah Winfrey

"The final forming of a person's character lies in their own hands."
–Anne Frank

Breath of Life

Heather Schultz

"One, two, three, breathe! "One, two, three, breathe!" Cardiopulmonary resuscitation (C.P.R, a medical procedure performed to restore breath and therefore life to a person who is dying) is done everyday all across America to all people of different ages and races.

Imagine yourself in this situation. You are walking along the edge of a lake, when suddenly you hear a strangled cry. You turn, and see that someone has fallen into the lake - someone who can't swim. His head disappears beneath the churning water, cutting off another terrified shout. Arms flailing up and out, water spitting from his mouth as it fills his lungs, he reappears, but only for a moment. You witness this person losing his battle to survive. Your eyes lock with his. Your own body shudders with sheer panic. You have become, willing or unwilling, this persons only link to life. You are his last hope. In a final surge of energy, his arms extend, fingers spread taunt reaching for anything or anyone who may pull them from this unimaginable place.

Here is the question - the only one that really matters. Do you reach out? Do you jump in? Do you perform CPR? For myself, that answer is yes. As a registered nurse, CPR instructor and former paramedic I have performed CPR on another human being. I have brought another person back to life. This is an incredible feeling and a powerful gift.

In fact, when faced with that kind of emergency, I believe most people would go to great lengths to save someone. Fortunately, you probably will never be called to perform CPR. In other ways, however, we are called to breathe life into other people every day.

There are people in your school, your work place and your community who are drowning. They may not be in the water but they are in danger. They may be drowning in despair, abuse, neglect, drug abuse or loneliness - because they don't feel accepted, popular or even liked. Many people who appear completely alive are drowning; they are simply doing it more slowly.

A human spirit is at stake. We must reach out. We must jump in. Each of us has the ability to breathe life back into another human being. Every time a person crosses your path you have a decision. Will you uplift this person's spirit or will you destroy their spirit. You can breathe life back into another person; your resuscitation technique may be as elegantly simple as a smile, a kind word, a gentle touch or a nod of affirmation. Don't wait for tragedy to claim another person. Jump in now. Reach out today.

I want to leave you with this challenge: Live everyday striving to uplift rather than destroy. Choose your words with caution. Be kind. Be careful. Be positive. Be there.

Appreciation Makes a Difference

Shaun Hays

A young man was helping me set up for a program as it was his duty to do every weekend for five months out of the year. He did such a great job for me and made life so much better. One day I wanted to sincerely acknowledge him and show my gratefulness for his services. I put my arm on his shoulder and said, "I want to thank you for all you do, it makes such a difference, thank you."

Tears swelled up in his eyes. I asked what the matter was. He shared that I was the first to show any appreciation for all his efforts. Who ever he worked for, he never received any feedback as to if he was doing good, but only feedback to everything he did wrong. It got so bad that he considered quitting many times, and the words of appreciation that I shared with him seemed to come at the right time.

I do not believe there is a wrong time to tell someone you appreciate him or her. Anytime is a good time. People hunger to know that they are doing well, and that the work they do is making a difference. Appreciation lets people know they are important and valued. We all hunger to feel that way. If we did not feel these things, why would we go day to day feeling purposeless? The sun could be shining, but for all you know, it is dark and grey out. Appreciation is like the sunlight to the soul. Make sure that your appreciation is sincere and real, otherwise it simply means you are doing it to serve your own motives, which is not good and lacks character.

A Positive Character Makes a Difference

Shaun Hays

Real Character is doing what is right, not what is popular. It is being honest with the little things. It is returning the missing wallet with all the money inside of it. It is going back to the cashier and telling him, "you gave me too much change". It is not gossiping behind someone else's back. It is not saying one thing and then doing another. Real Character is claiming responsibility for your actions, situations or even things that may seem unfair. It is stepping forward out of the crowds. Our character can be our attitude, it surely is our actions. It is persevering in tough times and not giving up. Character is not throwing temper tantrums, it is resolving to understand and find solutions that serve everyone. Character is how you treat others. Are you rude and vulgar, or uplifting and truthful? Do you follow through on what you say, or do you let it linger? Do you get defensive if someone gives you wisdom or do you listen and learn? It is thinking before acting on impulses to buy junk. It is having the courtesy to pick up trash on the ground and put it in the dumpster ...even when it is not yours. It is respecting yourself and others. It is how you treat property which is not yours. It is how you spend your time. It is how you treat your girlfriend, boyfriend, mom, dad, brother, or sister.

This is only the tip of the iceberg. Character is the very core of who we are. Real character equals real success. It means you are not fake; what you see is what you get. Building a strong foundation of character starts by asking questions like: Is this right? What is the right thing to do? What is the right way to act in this situation? Doing this is the starting block. Building character is not a 50-yard dash. It takes time, sometimes years. Habits build our character. And building habits take time.

Character is doing what is right even when you think no one is looking. Others are watching you to see if they should follow your example. You cannot walk right, yet talk left. It just won't work. Having a solid character is being responsible. Character is not being popular. It is doing what is right! Character is not your looks or anything on your outside. It is the core of what you stand for. It is what you will do in tough situations, how you respond to life. It is who you are. You can fool others some of the time, but you cannot fool yourself. You are your character.

The number one key to all success today boils down to character. Can people trust you at your word? Will you do what you really say? Character is found rooted in our actions when others are watching us and when they are not. If a camera were on you all the time for the world to watch, like in the movie The Truman Show, how would you live? The key to a solid character is deciding what needs changing, what needs improvement, what is your definition of values and morals that you will stand on, no matter what? Once you define your character, then walk in it. Practice it everyday - in little things and big things. Character counts for everything.

Laughter in Disaster Makes the Difference

Johnny Beede

"One of the best things people can have up their sleeves is a good funny bone!"

"Let's paddle something fierce!" I cried out. Fifteen people hollered in approval. I was second-in-command leading a 25-mile whitewater trip down the Nooksac River in Washington State. Rapids the size of Volkswagen Bugs, as well as fallen trees, and submerged rocks all awaited us.

Kevin, my boss, was nervous. It rained the night before, and the river was faster and rougher than usual. After a few hours, the raucous rapids were hurtling our eight aluminum canoes like ping pong balls stuck in a jumbo-jet turbine! My boat was half-filled with water. My partner was frantically bailing water as I steered clear of tree-stumps and beaver dams...and we weren't even at the toughest part yet!

"PORTAGE!" Kevin yelled so loud that bears must have covered their ears. Portage means, "Get to shore *now* and carry your boat. It's too dangerous to continue." We went to shore.

One boat missed the command.

"Get to shore now!" I was running along shore, trying to keep up with them. "Get to shore now!" It was too late. THUNK! The canoe broad-sided a log-jam and flipped upside-down. Both passengers, Mike and a guy we called Tarzan, were sucked underwater with the canoe!

Unbelievably, Mike popped out of the water 25 feet down stream and swam to shore. Tarzan managed to pull himself out from under the canoe and get on top of the logjam.

The canoe was gone. Mike was safe. Tarzan was sitting on the logjam with rapids on both sides of him! He was safe as long as he stayed put because logjams are solid. But Tarzan started to panic and looked like he was going to jump into the water. We had to settle him down quickly, but we were a hundred feet away.

Kevin yelled over the rapids, "Hey Tarzan! The canoe is coming out of your next paycheck!" A joke, at a time like this? I couldn't believe it. We could see the white of Tarzan's smile. Kevin yelled, "Show us your muscles!" Tarzan started flexing in the middle of the river! "Tarzan, give us a war cry!" Tarzan beat his chest and let out a holler. He relaxed and waited for us to rescue him.

Kevin and I got in a canoe and paddled like crazy to get to the crash site. We picked up Tarzan and safely finished the trip with seven canoes.

I later asked Kevin why he made a joke. "Tarzan was in a panic. The best way to stop panic is to use humor because laughter lowers your heart rate and blood pressure. If you don't laugh, you might as well be dead." Kevin's sense of humor probably saved Tarzan from drowning.

You too have a sense of humor. You may not be able to use it in life-and-death situations, but use it daily...hourly...minutely! There's a ton of people who feel like their hearts are drowning in the torrent of life. The quickest way to help them is to crack a joke! Laughter releases 'endorphins' into the brain which reduce stress, sharpen wit, help you to think clearly, and may even have healing properties! So smile constantly. Make sure not to make-fun or laugh at other people's expense, but by all means, laugh, play. You never know who you may give hope to. Emerson wrote, "If you would rule the world quietly, you must keep it amused." The same goes for making a difference. Keep the world amused.

Hope Makes a Difference

Heather Schultz

Your fingers are crossed. Your heart is racing. The anticipation is almost unbearable. You can't stop wondering: will it turn out the way I hope? Most people rely on hope, probably more than they realize. After all, have you ever said, "I hope I pass my test" or "I hope I get this job" or maybe "I hope Mom doesn't find out?"

Hope helps us deal with our everyday lives, and in times of unusual turmoil. Hope can actually be a life-changing force. Hope can bring direction to your life and help you find answers when you have questions. You can lean on it in times of doubt. Perhaps most importantly, hope gives you a reason to go on. And that is when miracles happen.

I was recently reminded of the importance of hope. In 1999 I was pregnant with my first child. My husband and I were thrilled to be starting our family. Excitement turned to concern at 25 weeks into my pregnancy when I developed a life threatening medical condition. The doctors told me they must perform an emergency c-section. When my baby was delivered she weighed just over a pound and she fit into the palm of my hand. She was the size of a Beanie Baby. The doctors were not very optimistic. I remember the day her neonatologist said he did not expect her to live over two hours. They told my husband and me to prepare ourselves for the worst and to be ready for a goodbye. We chose to hope for the best. Two hours passed, then a day, then a week and a month. She spent several months in the intensive care unit. When she came home, she weighed only four pounds. Today she is happy, healthy, sassy and very much alive. Oh, and now she weighs 28 pounds!

Please don't ever let anyone tell you that hope doesn't exist. It does. Miracles do happen. I have one in my life and her name is Liberty Alexis Schultz.

I wish to leave you with this little piece of hope. It was Christmas day. Liberty had only been home from the hospital a few months. She was lying in my lap when she sneezed. I said, "Oh, God bless you." My four-year-old niece climbed in my lap and said, "Aunt, Heather. He already has!"

Gabe Will Dance

Andy Thibodeau

"If you could do something to improve the quality of your child's life, wouldn't you do it?" This is the simple answer that my friend Tonya gives when asked why she had expensive surgery on her unborn child. To all of us who seek to make a difference in the world, her statement, and the story of Gabriel William Schleihauf, demonstrates the power of people coming together to improve the quality of someone else's life.

It was a few days after we celebrated my birthday in January 2002 that Alphonse, my wife, and his wife, Tonya, received the phone call that changed their lives. Tonya, pregnant with their third child, was told that the baby would be born with spina bifada. The disease in its simplest terms is an opening in the foetus' back which allows fluid from the uterus to damage the spine. Children born with the disease do not usually gain the ability to walk, can be unable to control their bowel functions, and often need a "shunt" to drain the continual build-up of fluid in the skull into the stomach. It was a devastating announcement to Tonya, Alf, and all of their family and friends.

Devastation turned to hope and resolve, when an option was presented to them. Through a combination of Internet research, the insight of friends, and a Discovery channel program, they learned of the work of Dr. Bruner and Dr. Tulipan at Vanderbilt University in Tennessee. These doctors had been operating on spina bifada babies while in the womb to close the opening in the spine and minimize the damage. However, the surgery was expensive at $50,000 US (almost $80,000 Canadian), it is not covered by health insurance, and this would be only the 150th operation of this type. Alf and Tonya felt that since Vanderbilt is located within an hour's drive of her parents' home, this was the "sign" that they needed to put faith in the surgery. Just three weeks after the diagnosis, Tonya was being operated on at Vanderbilt. Then we had to wait. They would not know if the surgery had been successful until the baby was born. In the meantime, there was a chance of miscarriage, so Tonya had to adjust her lifestyle to lessen the stress on the baby.

It was a tense time between January and late April; yet, it was also at this time that Alf and Tonya realized the strength of the love and support around them. Tonya told me how they were amazed at how many people shared in their desire to make a difference with this unborn child. Listing to their actions is inspiring! In Tennessee, Tonya's family provided two weeks of accommodations while they went through the surgery procedures. They cooked meals, helped with the kids, and donated money. Churches that Tonya had attended while growing up came together to help. They arranged bake sales and asked for donations from passing vehicles. An amazing $20,000 was raised! For Alphonse, his most memorable moment happened as he drove back alone from the Detroit airport to Canada after the surgery. His credit and bankcards had accidentally been magnetized and ruined while he was at the hospital. He arrived at the border with no money to pay the toll for the bridge. They finally let him across. When the customs officer on the Canadian side asked "anything to declare," Alf spilt his guts to the agent as if he were a patient on a psychiatrist's couch. He talked about the stresses of the surgery, of leaving his wife and children in

Tennessee for two weeks, and of how he had run out of money because his cards were not working. The customs officer reached out and handed Alf a five dollar bill and simply said "go get yourself some lunch. Welcome home." Difference makers can appear in the most unlikely places!

Alf's family, church and many friends in the London area helped by providing babysitting, cooking meals, cutting the grass, visiting the hospital and giving constant emotional support. The church which the Schleihaufs had been members of for only three months, brought tears to Alf & Tonya's eyes when they presented the family with a $5,000 check. "We were just amazed at these strangers who cared about us and our baby," Tonya told me.

A highlight of our efforts here was the organizing of a silent auction and dance on April 20. It was in the process of organizing this event that the Schleihauf's decided to name their unborn boy Gabriel (after the angel) with a middle name of Will (for William). Thus the name of the dance reflected our goal and our belief for the baby: Gabe Will Dance. The money raised would pay for the surgery that will allow Gabriel to dance in the future. The auction items were donated and everything including the hall rental, the food and the DJ was provided free of charge. Two hundred people attended this amazing evening of family, friends and fun that raised over $12,000!

One week later, Tonya was rushed to the hospital with contractions. Just when it looked like she was going to be spending almost three months in the hospital, Gabriel arrived in the world ten weeks premature on April 29. He was a surprisingly healthy 4 pounds, 4 ounces...and he was kicking his little legs!

The surgery was a success! The effort and love of so many had made a difference. Gabe WILL dance.

Enthusiasm makes an AWESOME difference!

Aaron Davis

"Fires can't be made with dead embers, nor can enthusiasm be stirred by spiritless men. Enthusiasm in our daily work lightens efforts and turns even labor into pleasant tasks."
James Mark Baldwin

Bright and early each morning my two little boys come dashing down the stairs at break-neck speeds to begin another day full of excitement, adventure and unlimited playtime (at least until afternoon nap time). After a full-day of fun, fights and whatever else they find themselves into its back up to bed for a good nights' rest. When its bedtime for the boys at the Davis Household you would think that my wife and I were forcing our boys to eat sour lemons accompanied by hot-sauce! They cry and complain endlessly! They are even pretty good at the stalling technique in which they will ask us to read the entire Bob the Builder collection right at bed time, hmmm? As I finally make my way back downstairs from their room I can't help but smile at the enthusiasm those two little guys have for the blessing that we call Life! They can't wait to get out of bed in the morning and they dread the arrival of nightfall!

Hundreds of people wake-up each morning with a frown on their face at the arrival of another day and thrilled to finally hit the pillow at night because of their lack of enthusiasm about life. The person who lacks enthusiasm for life is a miserable sight to behold. They seldom smile, they walk slower, and they constantly complain about their job, children, spouse, school and anything and everything else that comes within an inch of their space!

Enthusiasm is the difference! The person who genuinely believes that life is a tremendous blessing can't help but radiate with enthusiasm! Those who truly appreciate life and its vast opportunities and blessings walk with and talk with purpose and most importantly they live with a purpose. How does one begin to live with enthusiasm? You must saturate your mind with all of the great things that bring purpose to your life, such as your friends, family, and faith! Revisit your dreams and write down your goals. Do the things that you have been putting off because you lacked the enthusiasm to even attempt them. As you read this think about the awesome privilege it is to have the ability to read and intelligently organize your thoughts as you ponder the thoughts from this very book! Years ago the famous psychologist William James introduced his "As if" principle. He said, "If you want a quality, act as if you already had it". Friends begin acting as if you already lived a life full of enthusiasm and I guarantee that you will begin to develop a life full of joy, fullness, and a continual appreciation for each day!

Each morning I greet the day with thanksgiving and with the attitude that "Today is going to be MY DAY"! I seize the day from the start. You may be reading this and saying to yourself "Come on Aaron, what about those mornings when you say to yourself "forget all that enthusiasm mumbo jumbo". Do I awaken *every* morning with enthusiasm? Of course not! But I have to make a decision the moment my eyes open, either I can decide to seize the day with enthusiasm or I can get up with a major chip on my shoulder and scowl at everyone and anything. It doesn't matter what side of the bed you get up on, it only matters what attitude you decide to have!

The Difference Maker in the Mirror

Patty Hendrickson

Who are the difference makers in our lives? Who are the people that magically change our world? Let me share with you a difference maker that I like to have around. Every once in a while this person catches me by surprise and does some wonderful things. I sometimes get used to the beauty of this person simply making a difference. Then this person disappears and I wonder where she is hiding. I think you've met this difference maker or one that is very similar.

The difference maker is so close to you. Stand up and walk to the nearest mirror. Look at this miraculous difference maker. See him. See her. Yep, that's a real honest-to-goodness difference maker in the flesh. That difference maker has the potential to do so many amazing things. Let me tell you a little bit about that difference maker . . .

The person staring at you in the mirror remembers some wonderful times of being a difference maker –

Once you were behind a woman in the check-out line whose child was screaming. The woman's expression looked as if she too wanted to scream. The difference maker in the mirror started making silly faces at the child and the child stopped screaming. The woman may or may not have thanked the difference maker, but you made her life easier.

Once you were at school and the quiet, shy kid who rarely enters a conversation looked very sad. You noticed that sad kid because you often notice him. The difference maker in the mirror saw this quiet, shy kid, smiled at him acknowledging that he saw he was sad. The quiet, shy kid felt so much better because someone looked into his eyes to acknowledge he was sad. The quiet, shy kid may not have thanked the difference maker, but you made his life a little better that day.

Once you were at home where your mom was very busy and pretty stressed out. That day the difference maker in the mirror went to the bedroom and without any requests put away some stuff that was on the floor. It wasn't very fun but you did it without being asked. Your mom may not have thanked the difference maker, but you made her life easier that day.

Once you were at school and your teacher was very frustrated with a class that was very loud and rambunctious. Everyone in the room seemed to be talking for no reason other than to make the loudest noise possible. The difference maker in the mirror made the decision to not start talking to other people. Instead the difference maker in the mirror gave a few looks of disapproval to other students nearby. The teacher may not have thanked the difference maker, but you made her life easier.

Each of these times the person you see in the mirror chose to be a difference maker. More importantly, the person in the mirror chose to be a positive difference maker. We have the choice to be a positive or negative difference maker. Every encounter we have with another human being gives us this opportunity. Every where you go and every one you meet offers you a unique opportunity to be a difference maker. The question to ask yourself today and everyday is so simple – Are you going to be a positive difference maker?

Go ahead ask the person in the mirror. You are such an amazing difference maker!!

The Voices at My Back

Scott Greenberg

BANG! The gun fired and the Los Angeles Marathon began. 23,000 runners vied for position, the more elite pushing forward through the crowd. I took off at a fast clip and scoffed at the dawdling turtles falling behind me. I trained hard and was in good shape. This was my day. I knew I wouldn't win this race, but I'd leave plenty in my dust.

For the first hour and a half I glided like a gazelle through Los Angeles' South Central District. My knees were pumping and my fists were swinging. At the tenth mile marker I checked my watch and realized I was making great time. Up ahead was a quarter mile uphill and I was hungry to attack it. I eagerly threw myself up the incline, not prepared for what waited for me at the street's peak.

Like a bolt of lighting, my right knee was struck with a sudden, excruciating pain. I staggered, then limped downhill and tried to regroup. "OK, this is just one of those temporary running pains," I dismissed. "I can run through it." And so I did.

But the pain increased. I realized this wasn't an ache. This was an injury. Now the only run I could manage was a quick hop on my left foot, and a delicate limp with my right. I hobbled passed the 12th mile marker and did the math – more than 14 miles to go.

As I pondered the long road ahead, I became aware of my own body weight and strained breath. More and more runners sped past me. I actually felt like I was moving backwards. Would this race ever end? I was broken, and there was no going on.

And that's when I heard them.

Cheerleaders - not girls in skirts - but people, thousands of them lining the streets, screaming, encouraging, "You can do it!" "You're almost halfway there!" "You're going to make it!" It was a cacophony of support. As my disability became obvious, more and more cheers were directed at me. An invisible person put a cup of water in my hand. Another gave an orange slice. At one point a mist of water was sprayed in my desperately tired face.

Every voice propelled me one step forward. For 14 miles these angels sung to me, their tender, passionate voices drowning out the cries in my head. I succumbed to their power and just let my body finish the race. With a wounded knee and a melted heart, I crossed the finish line.

My body ran the marathon, but the love of over one million spectators made it possible. They didn't have to cheer. They chose to. They were selfless, caring strangers who volunteered to be the wind at my back. The medal draped around my neck was a reminder that you can't have accomplishment without encouragement. I was not proud when I crossed the finish line. I was blessed.

The Powerful FORCE of Encouragement

Some people refer to me as a motivational speaker. I like to see myself as a master of encouragement. I've seen the power of encouragement do some pretty awesome and amazing things. There is an unexplainable force that makes a difference when we give encouragement. It is a like a light of hope that shatters through the skin, and wiggles through the darkest regions of a person's life. It travels swiftly for it knows its mission and destination – the heart! When it reaches the heart it fights off everything negative; doubt, tough times, mistakes, whatever is hindering a person from their best. Encouragement heals the heart, lifts people up, pulls them along, pushes them up, and gives them the touch that makes a difference!

Encouragement costs
nothing to give.
Encouragement brings out
the best in others.
It builds people up.
You can never go wrong
when you encourage
someone.

When you extend a hand to others and ask, "What can I do for you?" You will always have friends, and work, and you always make a difference.

You cannot always repay others for the things they do for you, but you can repay them by doing something, anything for someone else.

You've Got What It Takes

Kathleen Hassan

It was my very first National Speakers Association meeting. I was brand new and scared to death and yet I felt as if I'd arrived home. Here was a roomful of people who actually got what I was trying to do with my life.

One of the sessions was a storytelling workshop. The presenter led a visualization exercise to help us remember our stories, and explained that stories help anchor the learning for our audiences. During our guided meditation, he had us picture ourselves in our family car, driving down the street of our childhood home. He encouraged us to remember vivid details, so we dug deeper, picturing the inside of the car, the dashboard, and the steering wheel. One woman raised her hand and said, "What if you can't remember the inside of the car?" and he responded, "Just pull into the driveway."

At that exact moment I was whooshed back in time and suddenly I was sitting in the car with my mother. I was sixteen years old and I was next to my mother in the passenger seat when we pulled into our driveway. My mother turned to me with the saddest eyes I've ever seen. She spoke so quietly I thought I had misheard that the doctor had just told her she had less than a year to live unless she had open-heart surgery.

After the session, I went up to the woman who had asked that question and I thanked her for jogging my memory and told her about my recollection. I went on to tell her that my dad had died when I was ten and that my mother died having open-heart surgery when I was only sixteen years old. I babbled on about being brand new to the speaking business and how I knew that I'd been called to do this work. I said, "I don't have my business cards, topic, niche market or anything. All I know that I have a burning passion to help others live a healthy life."

She asked, "Are you a member of the National Speakers Association yet?"

I blurted out, "It costs $500 to join the National Speakers Association!"

She grabbed my hand and said, "Come with me!" She marched me through the hotel lobby, up the stairs to her hotel room. She took out her checkbook and wrote me out a check for $100.00 and said, "If money is the only thing from stopping you from becoming a member of the National Speakers Association, here is one-fifth of your dues. I want you to work hard to make the other four-fifths, because you belong here and you've got what it takes." The woman's name is Marcie and she was the very first person who saw something in me that I hadn't even begun to see in myself.

I've been growing my speaking business gradually over the last seven years and it has blossomed into the most rewarding career I ever could've imagined. This year I was invited to speak at the National Speakers Association's Youth Conference in Orlando, Florida. The youth in the audience ranged from age ten to sixteen – the exact same ages I was when I lost my dad and mom. I had been preparing my whole life for this moment and I chose Marcie to introduce me. My message was a simple one. Each of us has the power to make a difference in someone else's life. Five little words that changed the course of my life forever: "You've got what it takes."

Power in Its Purest Form

Harriet Turk

I will never forget Alex. I met him when he was in third grade and I was teaching Vacation Bible School. He had the biggest dimples and the cutest smile. He was one of the oldest kids in my group of seven, and I pegged him as a group leader. He just looked the type.

I was right. He was a leader; just not the type I was looking for. To Alex, everything was stupid. The games, activities, stories, snacks— you name it, it was stupid. No matter what we did, he didn't like it. I kept trying and trying to turn his attitude around, but it did not work. Once, when we were playing a game, Alex just quit. It didn't matter to him that he made his partner lose; he just got mad that things weren't going his way and he quit. Soon, other boys in the group started to follow his lead. Suddenly, they didn't want to be my helpers, they didn't play the games, and they started imitating Alex's every move.

Alex was a strong leader. He had influence, respect and ultimately he had power over the majority of my group. Obviously, one can be just as powerful when he is negative as one can be when he is positive. I was freaking out. My sweet, little group was in shambles and I did not know what to do! Finally, I figured it out.

I needed Alex. I needed him on my side. Trying to run a successful group without his support was just _not_ going to happen. I did the only thing I knew to do. I took him aside and begged him, (yes, I begged him) to help me. I told him I could not run this group without him and I needed his help. I told him it was my first time to teach VBS (I knew he had been coming for a couple of years) and I was lost. What could he do to help me? What did he think would make the group activities better? Almost immediately, my life improved.

Alex had TONS of ideas. Some were great and I used them, some were not so good and he compromised. I ultimately got all my ideas and plans into action and Alex believed he came up with most of them. What changed? Alex suddenly felt important. He had a purpose. All Alex wanted was to _feel_ important. When he felt important, his attitude improved. I could have fought him all day long and tried to run the group my way. However, I knew I would lose. He was too powerful.

During that week I learned a very valuable lesson. I may have been the designated leader, but Alex was the real leader. Although he didn't have the support of all the team, he had the majority. Without his help, I would have lost the battle. The greatest part for me was when I gave him a little I gained a lot. By giving Alex purpose, I achieved my goal of having a great team.

If you are in a leadership position and you continually butt heads with someone who seems more powerful, you will ultimately lose if you do not gain that person's support. Difference makers and true leaders know how to get their team behind them. It can be a long, slow process, but ultimately the team benefits from the shared leadership.

You may be the designated leader of a group but it does not automatically mean everyone will readily follow you. Your attitude mixed with flexibility will help win over the negative influence. Those two ideas are leadership in its purest form. You need every group member to participate. You want your goals to be achieved. Knowing how to use your intuition, communication skills and your connections will make the difference.

Excellence Makes a Difference

In all you do....

Sam Glenn

Learn to serve with an attitude of excellence. This shows you are committed to providing the best for your family, friends, and customers. All of us are in the business of serving, whether you work behind a desk all day, answer phones, travel, sell, preach, clean floors, educate, whatever you do, you are in the business of serving. To serve is an act of real love, says my friend Larry Winget. Love what you do with a passion, and the results will be evident in the way you serve others.

If you hate what you do, you will never be excellent at it and you will always sell yourself and others short of your best. When you provide great service to others, without taking advantage of them with the purpose of personal gain, your rewards will be the best that life has to give. To serve others in what we do with character is an honorable action that benefits all involved.

"Do you see a man skilled in his work? He will serve before kings; he will not serve before obscure men."
— Proverbs 22: 29

If you do average things, you live an average life. If you do excellent things, you live an excellent life.

The opportunity to touch the life of another with love,

care, and encouragement might come when you least expect it. It might come through a hug, a prayer, the right words, a phone call, who knows. But I will say this, when we give our best encouragement and love to others it is always enough to do the job. It is better than nothing, and counts for everything.

My Story of "Watts"

Shaun Hays

I once took a street person from the proj-
ects of Chicago, to an affluent suburban
church, on his request. It shattered so many
stereotypical borders for me. I really thought,
he, and the people he would meet, would disgust each other. Instead, I witnessed understanding.

"Watts," as he liked to be called, had a
hunched-over frame, but came with his best
smile on. He said he'd found a place to wash
his clothes and take a bath, but honestly you
couldn't tell. His crooked hand pulled the cap
from his head, to show respect. By doing this,
he revealed three unkept dreadlocks and a
few blades of brown grass twisted among
them.

In sharp contrast was the young lady down
the row. She had long hair, and a long new
dress. Her bible was large and covered in
pink material with a little lace around it. Her
innocent eyes glues forward. To my amaze-

ment, (and horror) Watts moved down the row to share the young lady's "big book." She didn't act skittish or react in disgust. She smiled enthusiastically, and held the book where he could see it. When the collection plate was passed, Watts stood up and dug for a coin he had been saving. I was amazed, because those of us who have "good lives" seldom do as much.

A group from the church did a skit that day that couldn't have been any more perfect.

- ❦ A man walks along the stage confident and happy.
- ❦ Someone tells him he's ugly. He feels ugly.
- ❦ Someone tells him he's stupid. He feels stupid.
- ❦ Someone tells him he's hated….
- ❦ Then, he's crippled, and ignored.
- ❦ Finally, someone new finds him and tells him they love him.
- ❦ They pick him up, wipe his face, and tell him he's beautiful.
- ❦ They walk off the stage together.

I wanted to cry. They had just depicted the very life sitting in between this girl and myself. I found out later that young girl had never been to our church before, and I have never seen her again. Watts talked with a minister that day, but I didn't feel right asking him what they said. He seemed different the next time I saw him, though. Like the skit that Sunday. But I never saw him again.

I tried to find him, but no one seemed to know what happened. He got beat-up, I guess but after that he vanished. I was trying to be his friend, when someone else understood and made a difference. I'll never know, perhaps, if we ever made a difference in Watts' life, but that young lady made a difference in me, for sure.

Sacrifice Makes a Difference

A. Mosby

When you hear the word *sacrifice* what comes to mind? Most times we don't even like to hear it. We think we must give up something that we really want. We don't live in a world where sacrifice is an honored quality, but it is a very necessary element, if we are to make a difference in our lives, as well as in the lives of others.

When you think of it, all sacrifice is, is the ability to delay temporary pleasure for permanent joy and fulfillment. Modern culture leads us to believe that success is a hit record, becoming a movie star, a household name or some type of an overnight success. I have come to realize that the world knowing who you are is not nearly as important as those closest to you knowing who you are.

When I was sixteen I discovered I was pregnant. I had no idea what this meant, but the days and years to follow would teach me. Because I was not financially or emotionally prepared for such a responsibility, I was thrust into a life-altering situation. Many times I found myself working week after week only to barely survive. There were times when I would have $20 to last me from one paycheck to the next. It seemed no matter how hard I tried to get ahead, something would always come up. Tyrone needed pants or shoes or the car would need tires. The one thing that kept me going was knowing that hard times would not last forever and the future was going to be better for my son and me. As I learned to cope with the financial burdens I realized I had to also deal with the emotional toil. I'll never forget Tyrone's 7th birthday party. I was consumed with making the day special for him and even borrowed the money from my mom to pull it off. "What a great day!" I thought to myself as I watched Tyrone and his cousins having the time of their lives. Then time came to cut the cake so we sang happy birthday and Tyrone opened his presents. When he had finished and the kids were going back to play, my son turned to me and said "Mom, I'd have more fun if my dad were here." I was crushed! All I could think about was the fact that *I* was here, *I* had put this party together for him, *I* had sacrificed money *I* didn't have for him to have a great day, but he wanted his dad. I just looked at my son and nodded with a slight smile. I realized he didn't intend to hurt me. He was just being honest as any child would be. You see, we even have to sacrifice our emotions at times and trust that once again a brighter day is ahead.

Well, as the years continued to pass, my son continued to make me a very proud mother. He showed me one day that my sacrifice was not in vain, but paid the greatest of dividends. It was Valentine's Day and I was working late as usual. Tyrone was in his second year of college and doing great. He called me up on my cell phone and asked when I was going to be home because he wanted to stop by and use the computer. I said, "Son, you have a key. Just go by the house and use the computer. He said ok and then hung up. About fifteen minutes later he called me again and said, "Mom, when are you going to be home?", I said, "Tyrone, I don't know. Within the next hour or two, but you have a key so you can get in the house. He said ok and hung up again. Well he called a third time and said, "Mom are you coming home anytime soon?" I said in a rather harsh tone, "Tyrone, I am busy! You have a key. Just use the computer and do not call my cell phone again and I'll talk with you later!" So we hung up and about ten o'clock that evening I got home. As I entered the house, I caught sight of a dozen beautiful red roses on my kitchen counter. I thought to myself, "How sweet!" But wait it gets better. Under the roses was a box of chocolates. "Helllooo," I said to myself, "Now Tyrone, you are doing real good!" Oh, but let's not stop there! Under the box of chocolates was a card. On the front of the card it simply read "LOVE" and when I opened the card Tyrone had written a note that said, "Mom, I hope you have a happy Valentine's Day. And if you don't have a date, you can call me your Valentine." Oh, boy, tell me I don't know how to raise a terrific son!

It brings me such joy to share the Valentine story with you, because even then, at the ripe old age of 16, I realized that my circumstances were not going to be easy, but I knew I had to sacrifice to raise a son that I could be proud to call my own. Depending on what you decide and what you are willing to sacrifice, you can make any not-so-good experience a wonderful life-changing opportunity.

Do you want to make a difference in the lives of others as well as your own life? I can honestly say that having a child at such a young age is not the course you want to take.

I think you can see that sacrifice today, brings tomorrow's successes. Take the time today to develop and grow, so tomorrow you can have a bushel of roses waiting for you.

> Sacrifice is not a dirty word, but a life altering opportunity.
> Are you willing to give yourself the best life has to offer by having a vision for your future?

It Must Start with Me

Andy Thibodeau

In 1994, I met John Clarke, an assistant principal of a grade 7 to 9 junior high school in Calgary, Canada. He shared with me this story that perfectly underscores my message: making a difference starts with daring to care!

As John tells it, he was standing in the hallway, chaperoning the first school dance of the year. Another chaperone suddenly came running up to him, exclaiming, "John, you've got to come into the gym, right now!"

Fearing either the outbreak of a fight, or a couple dancing too closely, he raced into the gym to witness a touching sight. The grade 9 leadership class president had approached a girl in grade 7, a girl at her first ever dance, a girl he did not know, and had asked her for a slow dance. She was in a wheelchair. He had picked her up out of the chair and had held the girl as they danced. As he sat her back in the chair after the song ended, John asks us to picture the size of the smile on this young girl's face. Imagine how much she talked about that evening! In fact, she talked about it so much, that in grade 9, she was leadership class president. Where did she get her care?

I took two powerful morals out of this story. First, if care is contagious, it must start with me. That leader walked into the dance and took it upon himself to make a difference with someone that he did not know. As a true leader, he didn't concern himself with what others were doing to make a difference; rather, he entered the event concerned about what he could do. A second lesson is that to be a leader and make a difference, it doesn't take a big event, a moving speech, sports skills, musical talents, or model-like looks. Its simple acts of caring that often make the largest difference in the lives of others.

This was reinforced two years later when I was speaking at a high school student leadership conference in the Yukon, Canada. I soon got to know Elaine, a very special young lady who had been in a wheelchair all of her life. As part of my speech at the conference, I shared the "slow dance" story, encouraging the youth to dare to care. The next night, I was chaperoning the conference dance, when a student came to get me from the hallway. Pulling me into the dance, I witnessed one of the most powerful moments of my traveling career. It seems that a young man in grade 10 had listened to my message of "it starts with me". Almost the entire group of conference participants had formed a circle around one couple dancing. It was this boy, holding Elaine in his arms, slow dancing. As I joined the circle, Elaine's best friend was in tears beside me. "It's okay", I said to her, giving her a little hug. "Of course it's okay," she laughed through her tears, "Elaine's never slow danced before!"

Without a speech, without a planned event, without a special talent, this boy's simple act of caring had made a difference.

For me, that night was a huge inspiration to continue to speak to young people because they will listen and some will act. Dare to care, because it is contagious, but in your life, who starts it?

Conquering Your Fears Makes a Difference

A. Mosby

It's amazing what fear can do to a person, whether it's perceived or real. But the real problem with fear is that we can allow it to stop us from moving forward to achieve our dreams. Lots of times, we associate fear with pain so instead of even trying we'd rather not try in hope of avoiding pain. We concern our-selves with what others might think about us - if we have the ability to achieve what we desire or even if we do achieve our dreams, will we be able to live up to the expectation that come with succeeding? The truth is most people never really have to worry about these issues because they aren't even willing to try. I have learned that in order to take one step forward we must take a risk, and as Nike says "Just Do It!"

A few years ago my son, Tyrone, was playing in a basketball tournament. He road with the team, and I arrived a few minutes later. Once I got to the game, Tyrone came up to me complaining about a stomachache. I told him to just sit out the first half, and maybe he would feel better for the second half. It was brought to our attention that if Tyrone didn't play in the first half he would not be able to participate in the game at all. Tyrone said "No way, I want to play!" As the game got started, Tyrone was on the basketball floor holding his stomach and trying to run up and down the court. He was obviously in pain, but he pushed through it. As I sat there watching him I noticed a very interesting thing happen. When his teammate came down the court and threw the ball to Tyrone, he straightened up, grabbed the ball, took it down the court, and went for a lay-up. Immediately after he threw the ball up, he came down and grabbed his stomach. Luckily enough, his team won that game. What that experience taught me is Tyrone just didn't see a ball being passed by his teammate, he saw his dreams, his goals, his desires. He was able to put the pain aside long enough to do what he knew he had to do with the basketball to help his team to a victory.

Ask yourself, what do you do when pain hits you? What happens when you are disappointed; hurt because someone does not believe in you; scared of going after your dreams? Do you look that pain in the face and truly see your dreams coming toward you or do you just give into the pain and allow your dreams to pass? In order to make a difference in today's world, be willing to face your fears. We will be faced with challenges, with fears and with pains, but there will be those times when you must set the pain to the side for a moment and grab hold of our dreams. We are all scared of grabbing hold of our dreams, but the issue is not in the fear. What are you willing to do with it? I read once that cowards allow their fears to control them, while the courageous face their fears.

In order to be a difference maker, be willing to face your fears. Realize pain might be there, but don't let it stop you. Sometimes, be willing to move it to the side, if only for a moment, and then persevere. Go in the direction that is your true destination.

You Can Make a Difference by Keeping Your Mouth Shut!

Gina Waegele

Have you ever met someone who talks so much that you wonder if they are ever going to take a breath of air? Or, when they take a short breath, they start talking again so quickly that you can't interject a single word? As much as I hate to admit this, I tend to be one of those people who just talks. I admit, I am a recovering talkaholic. I began realizing the importance of listening rather than talking when someone told me that we were given two ears and one mouth for a reason.

One day, a friend was telling me about some problems he was facing. Before he finished telling me he said, "I don't need your advice. I just need you to listen and understand." Ouch. He knew I was going to follow up with some advice because I always have answers for my friends in need. What I found out that day is that even if I had the greatest advice to give, sometimes a listening ear is a better way to comfort for a hurting person.

I decided to put my new found knowledge to practice. A good friend of mine and I mentor a couple children. As we were discussing how we could help them in their situation, she asked me "How do you know so much about them? Why are they opening up to you and not me?"

I felt like telling her, "Because I listen." (My friend is a talkaholic too, but won't be quiet long enough for me to tell her she is.)

In this situation I committed myself to listen and ask questions to get the children to talk and express their feelings. Believe it or not listening, made a greater difference to them than for me to give them my advice and talk their ears off about what they should do.

To make a difference in the lives of others, listen to them. Discern when it is best to give advice and when to just keep your mouth shut! To all my fellow recovering talkaholics and to those who just admitted they are talkaholics, I know it is difficult, but try listening! I am finding a lot more satisfaction in learning from the words of others than just repeating everything I know. Even more so, I am now seeing that I can make a difference just by keeping my mouth shut!

The Lights On But You Don't Know

Josh Sosa

It was a typically hot summer day in Colorado. As I started to load the car with all the junk I needed to talk to teens about leadership. I opened the driver's side door and sat down. The heat hit me right between the eyes. Ready to feel the cool breeze of the air conditioner against my skin, I turned the key and guess what I felt? NOTHING, that's right NOTHING!!!! So I did what every man would do. I tried it again, and again and again. I guess I thought the car would change its mind and decide to start. Well, I was wrong. Finally, after about 20 minutes I gave up and went inside to call someone with jumper cables. I reached a friend and he showed up with cables. We proceeded to attach the cables and waited until my car was able to build up enough charge to ignite the engine. I got into the car and started looking for the reason behind this whole problem. As I searched for the problem I looked up and there it was. It wasn't an open door, it wasn't a dead battery. It was a little light about the size of your thumbnail. That is right! A stupid little light had made me late and had caused this entire ordeal. Once I was driving, I started to think about the whole situation. It then hit me between the eyes that this thumbnail sized light with only about two volts had the power to drain and stop an entire 900 pound car.

This is just like unresolved issues in our lives. In life, we get so caught up in dealing with the visual issues of our lives. So many people are more concerned with wanting to fix the things in their lives that everyone sees. They want to be happy, popular, energetic, full of life and exactly what everyone else in the world expects them to be. What they end up being is confused, lost, drained and lonely because they are busy fixing the external not the internal. Once you start working on your inside the outside comes naturally and people are drawn to you. It's normally not the big issues in your life that stop you in your tracks it's the small personal issues that are left unresolved and they end up creeping up on you when you least expect them to. They look identical to the little two voltage lights in my car.

On my fourth wedding anniversary, my wife gave me a plant as her anniversary gift to me. I guess that's what happens when you don't tell someone exactly what you want as a gift! Just kidding. Actually, it was a very cool plant. It had a cute little pot (my wife's words) and it was green and lush and it had a sign next to it that read, "Marriages are like plants...if left unattended they will die." The same goes for you and your lives. If you neglect to take care of your life on the inside you will begin to die (meaning you will lose your passion).

I Love Potatoes!

Harriet Turk

I absolutely LOVE potatoes! You can prepare them fried, mashed, au gratin, baked—I
don't really care how you cook them, just give
them to me! I could eat some style of potato
every, single day. So what's the big deal, you
ask? The big deal is I'm on a high protein, low
carbohydrate diet that does NOT allow me to
eat potatoes! What a struggle! The more I
think of <u>not</u> eating potatoes, the more I want
them!

Have you ever had that experience? You
want something so badly, you are not sup-
posed to have it, but the more you think of <u>not</u>
having it, the more you want it! To make matters worse, the more you try not to think
about it, the more you DO think about it! The
problem can be solved in a short amount of
time. Either you give in to your short-term

desire or stay the distance and achieve your long-term goal.

If I really want to lose weight, I'll resist the potatoes. If I just dream about losing weight, or sit and <u>wish</u> I would lose weight while eating a jumbo stuffed baked potato, I will never achieve my goal. I have to focus on what I <u>really</u> want (weight loss) and then have my actions match my words (resist potatoes!).

That is the hardest part—matching our actions with our words. It is also the most important thing we can do! True leaders in life state a goal AND follow through with action! Pretty hard to do, you say? It sure is. That's why I developed a system to help me. I will let you borrow it. Get a sheet of paper and pen.

Divide the paper in four equal sections by drawing three vertical lines. In the first column, write down all your goals, leaving a few lines underneath blank. In the second column, write down the date by which you want to achieve your goals. In the third column, write down the steps you will take to achieve your goals. Finally, in the fourth column, write down what is the price you are willing to pay to achieve your goals. What do I mean? I mean, what are you willing to <u>*sacrifice*</u> so you will achieve your goals? You might ask, "Who said anything about sacrifice?" "Ah, my little potato, that is the hardest part of all," I reply. For every desire, wish, goal or dream to be achieved, there is also sacrifice. I want to lose weight. I sacrifice eating potatoes. Even though I may not want to sacrifice, I have to.

For you, it might be sleeping while others party. It could be working when others play. It might be running while others walk. Whatever the desire, there is a price. While some goals come easy, others take a ton of hard work. That's where the burning desire comes into focus. If you have the burning desire to make a difference in your life, or in the lives of others, you will sacrifice something to meet that goal.

When you trade something you _want_ to do for something you need to do, you will be one step closer to reaching your goal.

Your Character Counts

Norm Hull

The content of your character is always determined by what you ingest. If you choose to put negative experiences into your personal database, then that is what you have to draw from later on in different situations. Character does not appear overnight or on a certain date or when you reach a particular age. It develops with each little and large act you do. There are plenty of instances when you will take three steps forward with your positive behavior and then negate the progress with one single act. Developing unshakable character is a journey, not a destination that is reached in one single trip.

When I was growing up there were plenty of temptations placed before my friends and me; you will have the same challenge as you make your way through LIFE.

It always is a constant struggle to think before you act, to listen before you speak and somehow be able to peer into the future so that you can visualize the result of any decision you make.

You can make the process of maturing easier by creating a solid bed of personal principles that you will never waver from, in any situation. I started a leadership camp 11 years ago and we have since based what we offer in our program on our CORE principles. If any activity or topic does not fit into these four areas then we do not include them in our camp. Imagine your life is like a camp, you get to decide which delegates get to attend, what you are going to talk about, which activities you are going to participate in and the memories you want to have when it is over. It is your camp so you get to make all the decisions and take all the responsibility that come with your choices. If you create a great camp you have nothing to fear. If a crisis pops up then you hopefully have prepared yourself to handle it based on the training, your experience and the people who you allow to be at your camp.

Your character is like a camp, you get to decide if you' re in charge of what comes into your camp or you can let someone else be responsible. There are plenty of people who are unhappy with the "camp" they have created but find it easier to blame someone else for what they created. You are your own camp director.

Unshakable character comes with experience, control of your own life and the willingness to always be responsible for your decisions.

Whose camp do you want to go to?

Your own because you know it is the best one because you created and made sure it was based on quality principles.

Go out and be the Character Director for your life. Because it is your life!

Get Involved with a Cause to Make a Difference

Gina Waegele

"Your life can impact many lives!"

One of the ways I have healed from my past life challenges is by volunteering in areas that have directly affected my life.

When I was in high school, I was a mentor to elementary students who have lost loved ones through death or divorce. Working with them helped me cope with my dad's death. I was also able to make a difference in their lives because I could empathize with what they had gone through.

After my sister was murdered by her own husband and after I left my abusive dating relationship, I learned that what we experienced was a lot more common than I thought. I learned that domestic violence is the leading cause of injury to women. I was not alone and my sister's case was not rare. Many people, mostly women deal with domestic violence as a part of their lives.

I began volunteering in a shelter for battered women and I worked with the children. I bonded with hundreds of different children throughout my years as a volunteer in the shelter. Some children were there for a day and some were there for months at a time. Then there were some who were in and out of the shelter several times throughout many years.

I remember a family that came from another state because their lives were in danger. One of the girls and I really bonded. After they had been there several weeks, I came in to work with the children and I barely recognized the young girl. Her mom dyed her hair and when I used her name when saying hello to her, she said, "No, Gina. That's not my name anymore. My name is now Gina." I laughed and said, "Yeah right." I thought, "How cute, she is pretending to have my name today."

An employee who worked at the shelter then told me that the family had to completely change their identities including their social security numbers to keep them safe and this girl had really changed her name to Gina. That was the last day I saw "Gina."

I don't know where she is, or what she is doing now. I still don't know what I did to have such an impact on this girl that she would change her name to my name. I do know that if I had not taken my tragedy and used it to help others, I would not have been able to make a difference in Gina's life or any of the other children's lives.

More importantly, they made a difference in my life in many ways. They helped me cope with burdens too large for a human to carry. They helped me heal. The children I have worked with and especially Gina were angels that made a difference in my life.

You can use your past experience no matter how tragic and make a difference in the lives of others.

The Losers Rule

Chris Bowers

Once, I led an exercise with 140, high school sophomores that had never met before. It was a "survival" type of activity where students have to instantly form groups consisting of a certain number of people. Extraneous people then get voted out of each group. To dismiss the extras, participants simply point at someone else and yell, "Get Out!"

Usually, one of two things will happen. The kids that are "out" feel dejected, and they either sit quietly until the end of the game, or they take great joy in seeing others become ousted. Some kids actually laugh and point at the other losers, because it makes them feel like less of a loser themselves.

This game was different. The first kid out was Geoff. Within seconds of losing, Geoff's personality emerged. When the next groups of kids were excluded, instead of laughing at them, Geoff greeted them enthusiastically. "Come on man," he yelled, "Join the LOSERS club!" Suddenly they didn't feel so bad. He then commissioned his loser buddies to induct the new losers into the Losers Club after each round. The quick ceremony included a hug and a loud cheer of "LOSERS RULE!"

I started to see some of the kids losing the game on purpose, because the Losers Club seemed more fun than the pressure of staying with the "in" crowd. Towards the end, the remaining players quit competing with each other saying, "Actually, it looks more fun to be a "loser." I was blown away. I had never seen it work this way.

The reason the game worked so well was because Geoff is a difference maker. Too often, we try to change the whole world, when really we should start by changing the person sitting right beside us. Geoff started by changing one person - convincing them that it was ok to be a "loser." Each person then began changing one other person. By the end of the activity, everyone had changed their attitude.

In the sands of life, you will look back and see one of two things, foot prints in the sand or butt prints in the sand. Foot prints are the positive impression we made on life and with our life. Butt Prints are the negative impression.

What will history remember of you?

We all have something to give that can make a difference. Each of us can lend a hand, give a hug, give of our time, make a phone call, get involved, clean toilets, pray with someone, do something. When we do that, do you know what? It all makes a difference! Who you are makes a difference. I have some new and good news for you: what you do and who you are for as long as you walk this planet does make a difference in this world. Don't keep your music and gifts locked up; open up and let the colors of who you are and what you have to give touch the life of another. When you give of yourself, you make footprints in the sands of life.

Three Attributes of a Leader with a Burning Heart

Frank Shelton, Jr.

In life, we can sit on the sidelines or we can get in the game of life and make a difference. Sadly, those in the stands are never satisfied. They either complain about how bad everyone is doing or they tell themselves repeatedly, "I wish I had tried out for the team." It is not wrong to pursue something and fail initially. It is wrong to fail because you did not try.

Remember, Abraham Lincoln had 11 public defeats for office in 27 years. What would have happened if Lincoln quit after his first embarrassing loss for county clerk in Illinois in the early 1800's? The world would have never known or benefited from the labors of arguably our greatest president. It has been said: "Our setbacks today can become our success stories tomorrow." Plus, what does not break us often makes us!

It has been said: "Anyone can make a living but it takes someone dedicated to make a difference." The world is filled with followers but leaders are rare. It has also been said that you are only a leader if someone is following you. The truth is that you can be a leader in both a positive or negative aspect. Hitler was considered a leader but his hatred attempted to wipe out a generation. Jim Jones was a religious cult leader who led thousands of followers to commit suicide. Osama Bin Laden led a handful of men to highjack planes on September 11, 2001, and changed the landscape of America forever. The biggest lie on the planet is that one life cannot make a difference. Friend, your life will make either a positive difference or a negative difference.

Listening Makes A Difference

Rick Minniefield

"People don't care how much you know until they know how much you care."

I went to a high school where there were roughly 2800 students. I can remember we had this hallway where all the good football, baseball and basketball players hung out during lunchtime. I was good in athletics, so I hung out in this hall during lunch. My buddy Myron was kind of like a class clown/comedian. Whoever came down that hall, we would make fun of them. Let me tell you about this particular day. We're sitting in the hallway and this young lady, Joella, was walking towards us. My buddy Myron goes, "Rick, Rick, Rick. Here comes Joella. Watch this, watch this", he said. As Joella gets a little closer, he shouts out, "Hey Joella, why don't you roll yourself down the hall, you'll get down here much faster". We all started laughing and gave each other high fives. It was hilarious. I looked over at Joella and saw that she was smiling and I said to myself, "Why is she smiling?" So I walked over and I said, "Joella, Joella, every single day we make fun of you and all you do is smile. Why is that?" She said, "You know what Rick, I don't want you guys to think you got the best of me. But as I walk through these double doors, I start to cry and I ask myself why don't you like me? Is it because I'm overweight? Is it because of the clothes I wear? Is it because I don't hang out with you guys? Why do you guys make fun of me, Rick?"

I didn't have an answer. I went to class thinking about it. I went to football practice thinking about it. When I got home, I asked my Mom, "Why do we make fun of people?" She didn't give me an answer. I went to bed thinking about it. I got up the next morning still thinking about it. I go to school; it's lunchtime and we are in hallway again. My buddy, Mryon yells out again, "Hey, Rick! Here comes Joella." It made me reflect when I was a child. I remember being afraid of the dark and every night before I would go to bed my Mom would read me a bedtime story. This one night she read Jack and the Beanstalk. After she got done, she gave me a little kiss on the cheek and said, "I love you son", and I said, "I love you Mom". She was getting ready to walk out of my room and turn the light off and I said, "Mom, Mom, what are you doing? Don't turn the light off. You know I'm afraid of the dark!" She says, "Babes you got to have courage", and I said "What does that mean?" I was just a little kid at the time. She says, "Babe, it means when you're afraid, you go anyway".

As Joella gets a little closer I begin to sweat. My buddies are getting ready to yell out a remark and I say to them, "Hey guys"! (I went over and grabbed Joella), "This is a friend of mine and we're not going to talk about her anymore". My buddies looked at me like I was crazy. "What do you mean we are not going to talk about her"? They got upset and they walked away. I went to the snack bar and grabbed two Pepsi's, one for Joella and one for myself. We sat down and talked. Actually, she talked and I listened. She said, "Rick you guys have been making fun of me ever since elementary school". I had a little smirk on my face. "Yes, we have." She said, "You know what? Every single day it hurt. Every single day, Rick. I'm starting to feel awful low. I hate coming to school". She goes on and on. She says, "My Mom, she's a single parent. When I get off of school, I have to go take care of my brothers and sisters because she works at night. I have to make sure they do their chores, their homework, and make sure they eat. Rick, I'm not having any fun being a teenager. Many nights, I think about killing myself". At this point, I start to cry. Why? Because I could have played a part in helping her kill herself. Because I was making life difficult for her. Our principal walked up and said, "Hey, what's going on out here?" I said, "I'll come see you when the bell rings".

The bell rings, Joella goes to class, and I go see the principal. I shared with the principal what happened. He sends a counselor to go see Joella. I go to football practice, my buddies ask me, "You're out there crying. What were you guys talking about"? I told them what happened. They said, "What can we do to help"? I said, "Why don't we take her to the Home Coming Dance"? They said, "What about our girlfriends"? I said, "Man, our girl-friends will understand". (They didn't.)

We went to the dance and had a great time. After it was over, we dropped Joella off at home. Two weeks pass, and she comes up to me, "Rick, I would like to run for student council. I said, "Great, I'll be your campaign manager". She said, "Ah, I don't need that, I don't care if I win or lose. I just want to say I had the opportunity". She ran and she won!

At the end of the year, we had our annual awards banquet. It's the last award of the night. It's called a Character Council Award and Joella is going to receive this award. As we're sitting there with all of our friends talking, our Activities Director walks up to the podium and starts reading off all these characteristics of this person. At the end, he asks, "Joella, will you please stand?" She gets up, she starts to walk to the podium, and as she's getting closer she starts to cry. She gets up there and said, "Thank you, thank you, thank you. Thank you for getting me involved".

I can't take credit for this story. It was up to Joella to make her own difference in her own life. But, what I can take credit for is this. I have been involved with leadership ever since elementary school, junior high school and high school. I've heard all the different types of Speakers. Went to all the different types of Leadership Camps. I was Mr. Leadership as I was growing up. But, you know what? I didn't get it. I didn't get until that day I actually sat down and looked into Joella's eyes and felt the pain I had been causing. A leader is somebody who lifts people up and not tear them down. A leader is somebody who encourages people to get the best out of life. A Leader is someone who listens to others. I didn't get it until that day and I'm thankful I finally got it. Otherwise, I wouldn't be in this book today. A Quote I have patterned my life by that has truly kept me being REAL is *"People don't care how much you know until they know how much you care."* We have to open up our hearts and our ears, and make a difference in people's lives that we come in contact with. I hope you enjoyed this chapter.

YOU Can Make it!

Sam Glenn

Sometimes in the pursuit of our dreams and the climbing over the mountains of challenges, the words YOU CAN MAKE IT are just what we need to hear in order to do just that - <u>MAKE IT!</u>

Many years ago when I attended the basketball camps for the Fellowship of Christian Athletes, there was a camp director there by the name of Bill Stutz. He was a giant, standing close to 6'9, with an attitude that reached about 10 feet high. Each morning all the campers had to do a warm-up run of one mile. I was not too fond of this. I hated this run and so did many of the overweight campers. I could run about 20 feet and call it a good day. The tough part was if you were one of the last to reach the finish line you had to do push ups. Let's just say I got pretty buff that week. There were a lot of chest and arm workouts that week.

As we would run this one mile, there at the finish line would be big Bill Stutz. He would be yelling with great enthusiasm the words, *"Come on! You can make it!"* He had a booming voice that carried the message not just to your ears, but to your heart. Hearing him yell those words, *"You can make it! You can make it!"* pushed me to keep going, even when I wanted to fall to the side of the road and quit.

When the campers ran past Bill, he would say, *"Good job. You made it!"* And he would congratulate each person who reached the finish line. As each camper passed the finish line, they too stood behind big Bill and shouted with the same enthusiasm, *"Come on! You can make it!"* I stand behind those words and I say to you, *"YOU CAN MAKE IT!"* Whatever you are going through, you can make it. Whatever loss you are facing, you can make it. Whatever mountain you must climb, you can make it. Whatever dream you are shooting for, you can make it.

Grandpa "Holy Buckets!"

Sam Glenn

Most called him Richard Albertson. For a short time, I called him Grandpa. My grandpa was a giant both in physical stature and in his attitude. He could make almost anyone smile and he had a special touch about him. Grandpa was a very special person and was always known for saying, *"Holy Buckets!"* Sometimes you could catch him singing a song that lifted you right up and made you feel REAL good.

Grandpa had his own special way with people. He had a touch of joy that he left resident in people's lives. He always seemed ready to help others out, or go the extra mile for you. If it was in his capacity, he would do whatever he could for you. That was his nature, or one that he acquired over years of learning and life's lessons. Everywhere I went with him, it seemed like everyone knew him, and had a kind word for him. And he had kind words in return. My grandpa was very approachable. He could talk to strangers like he knew them for years. He always expressed interest in people, and had a real passion for fishing with his grandsons. But if you ever got out of line, he would let you know. *"Holy Buckets!"* This is how I will always remember him. He didn't have a big organization that was out to change the world, he didn't go speak to large groups, he didn't even have that much money to give. But what he did have, he used and gave and that just seemed to be enough to make a difference. He, like all of us, had a unique touch about him. He used it well.

In 1989, my grandpa passed away due to lung cancer. He was sick for a long time and it always made me sad to see him breathing from an oxygen tank. In his last days, I remember seeing this giant of a man looking worn out and like there was very little life left in him.

At his funeral, many people showed up, some I knew and many I did not know. I listened to people tell stories about Grandpa and some even engaged in laughter. Some people wore expressions of happiness while others remembered him in tears. Watching all this made me realize something about life - one of life's greatest rewards. When people laugh, cheer, celebrate, give thanks, or remember you in tears at your funeral, it is not because you are gone, but because you touched their life. My grandpa touched many lives with who he was, the way he lived and what he gave. When you touch other peoples lives, life seems to give you back rewards beyond words, beyond money, and almost always beyond expression. It goes to the treasure chest in our heart.

This is YOUR Call to Action

Now is the time, this is the moment and you are the person...it is time to get up and do something. This is a call to action! Is there something you could do today that would contribute to making a difference in the life of another? Is there a cause or an issue that is burning in your heart and you want to do something...call to get information, interview someone, read about it, don't wait.

It is not enough to know that who you are makes a difference, you have to do something about it. Take action!

Take a moment to answer these challenging questions to get you going:

What is something burning in your heart?

What talents do you have that could be used to make a difference?

Is there something you have always wanted to try, but lacked the courage?

Who could you call or meet with that would be a great encourager to you?

What do you want to be remembered for?

What is one thing you could do today that could make a difference for you and others?

What would you like to learn or improve on?

Define your character–who you want to stand for and be known for?

What is something in your area or in the world that you believe needs to change or needs help?

How could you serve others better?

Define how you will respond to adversity? (You can do this, because it will define you.)

Is there anybody that would benefit from a prayer, a phone call, or an encouraging word from you?

What will history remember of you?

About The Authors

Sam Glenn

Some think Sam is crazy! He laughs like Scoobie Doo, walks like a Dinosaur, has a pet Chiwawwa, and is addicted to Krispie Kream Dounuts. But "ALL" would agree he is an awesome speaker! The bestest in the whole wide tri-city area of America. He is laugh therapy for your next event.

Sam is the author of 6 books, has spoken to audiences as large as 80,000 people. His message's focus on attitude, choices, and how to get a life if you don't have one.

Sam Glenn
(800) 818-6378
SamGlenn.com

Motivational Presentations
608 S. Washington Ste 101
Naperville, IL 60540

Andrea G. Mosby

"Speaking with Youth, about Youth, to make a difference in Youth"

Andrea has been speaking to youth for over 16 years. Her goal is to motivate, inspire and encourage individuals to look within to make the decisions that lead to their personal success.

Andrea is a natural with youth groups. She is awesome with teen assemblies, retreats, and leadership conferences.

Andrea G. Mosby
P.O. Box 7167
Denver, Colorado 80207

(303) 322-4029
hopeforkiddenver@msn.com
www.Christianyouthspeakers.com

Gina Waegele

Gina brings enthusiasm and excitement to audiences through her energy and attention grabbing demonstrations. In her programs, Gina communicates personal stories of triumph over tragedy as she shares entries from her journal, to personal experiences of domestic violence, to her one-of-a-kind experience as Miss Colorado. Audiences will cry and they will laugh, but most importantly Gina communicates through her words and through the way she lives her life, a message of hope and joy even in the most tragic circumstances.

Gina has spoken all over the country and shares inspiring stories along with important information ranging from relationships to motivation. She is the National Mentor Program Director at FRIENDS FIRST where she established peer mentoring programs across the country.

Gina Waegele
www.ginaspeaks.com
gina@ginaspeaks.com
1-800-909-WAIT

Frank Shelton

Frank Shelton is founder of "Frankly Speaking": Frank Shelton Ministries/Motivational Presentations. He is a native of Washington DC and is perfect for school assemblies, keynotes, graduation speeches, conferences, youth rallies and church revivals. At 30, Frank works fulltime on Capitol Hill and loves life and making a difference in the lives of others.

Frank Shelton
PO Box 742
Waldorf, Maryland, 20604

301-503-4440
shelton143@aol.com or
renee_franklyspeaking@yahoo.com
www.FrankShelton.com

Shaun Hays is a staff speaker and chalk artist with Sam Glenn Presentations, Inc. You can get info on him at samglenn.com. or e-mail him at shaunhays@hotmail.com. Shaun is best known for his Christian message, From Rebal Hill to Calvery Hill. He speaks at both Christian events and Leadership events. Sam Glenn highly endorses this program!

Harriet Turk

Since 1988, Harriet has worked with thousands of students encouraging them to live a healthy lifestyle, make positive choices and reach out to help others. She has her bachelor's and master's degrees in Criminal Justice and has worked as a probation officer, youth programs coordinator, traffic safety consultant, and a flight attendant!

Harriet is a versatile speaker who can develop programs for school assemblies, conferences, leadership retreats and peer counselor/mediation workshops.

Harriet Turk
338 Mysen Drive
Cordova, TN 38018

1-800-789-9559
Harriet@HarrietTurk.com
www.HarrietTurk.com

Chris Bower

Chris Bowers' life is dedicated to the positive influence and motivation of students through the use of humor. He is a dynamic storyteller and his hilarious tales serve to emphasize the lessons he is trying to convey. Chris speaks to audiences about the power they have to take risks and to have confidence in themselves. He uses humor to build camaraderie with students so he can encourage them to overcome their fear of failure and fear of what others may think of them. He emphasizes positive ways of dealing with frustration and conflict resolu-

tion. Audiences find themselves laughing along as he tells his own personal stories to get his points across. His presentations are dynamic and his enthusiasm is contagious.

317.201.5583
Motive8u@aol.com
www.WireInTheNose.com

Aaron Davis

Passionate, Humorous and exciting are some of the words that are used to describe the motivational presentations that Aaron Davis puts on for audiences of all ages throughout the nation. Individuals across the nation have sought the advice of Aaron because he has inspired them to take ACTION in their lives instead of allowing life to act on them. Aaron gains the trust of his audiences

because he speaks openly and honestly about his past experiences, which were nothing short of disaster. Aaron encourages his audiences to LOOK at the mistake, LEARN from the mistake, and then LEAVE the mistake behind and strive for greatness!! Aaron graduated from the University of Nebraska and he was also a member of the 1994 National Championship Football Team. Aaron is the founder of Truth Enterprises Human Development Co. located in Lincoln, Nebraska. Aaron and his wife Brooke reside in Lincoln, Nebraska with their two son's Aden four and Keenon 2.

Truth Enterprise Human
Development Co.
PO Box 81711
Lincoln, Nebraska 68501

1.800.474.8755
www.TruthEnterprise.com
ADavis@TruthEnterprise.com

Norm Hull

Norm's Leadership Training background spans over 20 years. As an International Consultant, Author, Speaker and Leadership Conference Director he focuses on group and personal development through education, humor and experiential learning. Norm is the CEO and President of The Leaders Forum A Training, Development and Leadership Company that works within the education and corporate arenas to create an environment for excellence and encourage people who want to take initiative.

The Leaders Forum, Inc.
39150 Madre Vista
Murrieta, CA 92562

Ph. (800) 722-6676
www.TheLeadersForum.com
Norm@TheLeadersForum.com

Andy Thibodeau

Andrew Thibodeau looks like he's 22 years old, but he's actually 32! For 10 years Andy has delivered thousands of fun presentations to schools and conferences across North America. Over 1 million people have seen him speak in all 10 Canadian provinces and 37 states.

Andy graduated from high school in London, Ontario, Canada. He then completed his college degree in history on the dean's honor list. His mission statement as a speaker is three simple words: "Make Care Contagious". You can reach Andy's Impact Presentations at 519-680-7332, www.andypresentations.com or e-mail: Talk2andyt@aol.com

Andy is addicted to ice cream and his best friend is his wife Elizabeth.

Andy Thibodeau
Impact Presentations
London, Ontario, Canada

Talk2andyt@aol.com
www.andypresentations.com
519-680-7332

Patty Hendrickson

For over 15 years Patty Hendrickson has been sharing her enthusiastic message throughout America and beyond. She is the author of the inspirational book - Who I Am Depends On Me! - now in its fourth printing. Patty is a Certified Speaking Professional, a designation earned by less than 500 people in the world. Patty's energy inspires, so her message sticks!

Patty specializes in leadership conferences and officer training. She most often speaks about leadership, teams and motivation.

403 Main Street
P.O. Box 508
Holmen, WI 54636

www.PattyHendrickson.com
Patty@PattyHendrickson.com
1-800-557-2889

Scott Greenberg

Scott Greenberg is a nationally recognized speaker and leadership consultant. He is the author of the Jump Start Leadership Workbook Series, and a contributing author to Chicken Soup for the College Soul. He has been spotlighted on national television and radio, and hosted a reality TV show pilot entitled For Better or For Worse for 20th Century Fox.

Jump Start Performance Programs
PO Box 3448
Van Nuys, CA 91407

(800) 450-0432
www.ScottGreenberg.com
Scott@ScottGreenberg.com

Kathleen Hassan

Teens, parents, teachers & business professionals alike have been inspired and motivated by Kathleen Hassan to turn obstacles into opportunities, to become who they were born to be and to live a life they absolutely love. Her message of self-worth, vision and personal power comes from her own life experience of turning tragedy into triumph. She helps people create a balanced life of peace, prosperity and true happiness.

Kathleen Hassan
P.O. Box 570
Milton MA 02186

877-370-1976
Inspire@KathleenHassan.com
www.KathleenHassan.com

John Beede

Speaker and comedian John Beede was born and raised in Las Vegas, Nevada. He developed his leadership skills by becoming an Eagle Scout, speech and debate state champion, class president, diving state champion and team captain, by achieving the National Forensics League's Degree of Special Distinction, and as a youth group leader of the Christian faith he is dedicated to. John is also a member of Phi Eta Sigma, Beta Theta Pi, and the National Society of Collegiate Scholars. He spent four summers as a wilderness team leader in Washington State's Cascade Mountains. Currently living in Chicago, Johnny now provides keynote talks, workshops, interactive sermons, and comic entertainment to groups like yours.

Phone: 1-702-809-2727
Email: johnny@johnnbd.com
Website: www.johnnybd.com

Mailing Address: Varies; refer to website.

Rick Minniefield

Think Big! Big Man! Big Heart! Big Smile! Big Messages! Big Changes for People!

Rick helps people realize they can achieve their goals and aspirations by learning some basic principles that build self-esteem and personal motivation. His presentations encourage, inspire and challenge people to take control of their lives and deal with difficult situations.

Consider Rick for Keynotes, Assemblies, Leadership Conferences, Prevention Programs and Baccalaureates.

RickMinniefield.com
Rick Minniefield
1584 Rue Francais
Chico, CA 95973
(530) 892 - 9273 Office Phone

Heather Schultz

Heather has spoken in 47 states and 7 other countries empowering millions. She will make you laugh and cry. She will educate, entertain and inspire you. But most of all she will make you think!

Heather's energetic presentations focus on building self-esteem, understanding the importance of making a good decision and leadership.

Heather's inspiring message leaves any audience from a school assembly to a youth leadership conference motivated, compelled to action and always wanting more.

3084 Castaway Lane
Atlanta, GA 30341

800-624-8939
Speakpeace@aol.com

Josh Sosa

Since 1996, Josh Sosa has spoken to teens all over the country. After he speaks, he sees a new passion among teens and a deep desire for change. Josh teaches that changed people, change people. Josh says, "We are a product of our own choices." The decisions that are made today have an effect on tomorrow.

Josh serves as the STARS Director for the Colorado FRIENDS FIRST Mentor Program. Through his one-on-one work, many teens have handed Josh their cigarettes and drugs and pledged to remain drug and alcohol free.

He speaks on many teen issues including sex and remaining abstinent with interaction and heart-felt stories–teens are captivated and challenged to make healthy choices. He also speaks on leadership and motivation.

Have you ever wanted to become a speaker and impact the lives of thousands?

Now you can, visit

www.speak101.com

Your future in speaking success awaits you.

Consider giving this book away as a gift...

To reorder this book, contact any author in this book or visit

characterspeaks.com.

Notes:

Notes:

Notes:

Notes: